MW01491998

DINGO DEVOTIONALS
Learning to Heel

by
Lynne Scott

Illustrations by
Ellie Miller

authorHOUSE®

AuthorHouse™
1663 Liberty Drive, Suite 200
Bloomington, IN 47403
www.authorhouse.com
Phone: 1-800-839-8640

First published by AuthorHouse 10/3/2007

ISBN: 978-1-4343-3153-3 (sc)

Printed in the United States of America
Bloomington, Indiana

This book is printed on acid-free paper.

Front cover photo and author photo by Karen Ward

All scripture references are from the
NIV version of the Holy Bible.

To all the people who work diligently to rescue dogs (and cats) from abuse and neglect. Their work is difficult, but they probably couldn't quit if they tried.

To all the grace-filled Christians who work diligently to reach others with the message of Christ's love and forgiveness. Their work can be draining. And they couldn't quit if they tried.

TABLE OF CONTENTS

SECTION TWO: THE DINGO

SECTION THREE: KENNEL DOGS

Preface

Obedience to God. That phrase made me run in the opposite direction. Fewer things sounded as dull and unappealing. Yet, in flaunting the constraints of God we inevitably become hostage to some other system of beliefs. Sometimes it is centered on a deity and sometimes on family. Perhaps it is staying busy to feel important, or accumulating the latest technological gadgets, or buying the most recent addition at the warehouse club for your backyard. While attending obedience classes with my dogs, I learned that God's "constraints" are actually liberating. They make life much more pleasant.

In class with Guinness, my Newfoundland mix, we watched as a particularly willful hound was put into an "enforced down." The trainer took the leash from the owner, stepping down on the leash four inches from the dog's training collar. The dog had no choice but to lay down. This dog was very dramatic and carried on. But it didn't rebel forever. Eventually, the dog got the message.

It was not in control. The dog changed and was a quick learner from there on out.

In that moment, as I watched that dog struggle, I knew exactly how it felt. I, too, was struggling.

When I took my second dog, Foster, an Australian Cattle Dog, through classes, I continued to see more parallels as I grew toward God. Then, in 1998, I started a boarding kennel. Daily, I thought of the adage, "All of life teaches biblical truth." And I saw this was true. And so began the Dingo Devotionals.

Introduction

New Year's Day, 2006. I was walking along St. Pete Beach in Florida. The day before, I'd flown down with friends to meet more friends there for a concert. It was excellent, and now to walk on the beach, out of the Ohio cold, was even better.

As I breathed in the balmy air, a surge of a strange emotion came over me. It was optimism. For the first time in over a decade, I looked upon the coming year with hope instead of dread.

I thought back to New Year's Day, 1991. I had the usual good-luck feast of roast pork and sauerkraut with my mother, father and brother, along with my fiancé, Darren, and his mother, father, brother and sister. The year had so much promise. Fifteen years later, death had taken all these men except my brother.

My father was killed by a drunk driver a few months before our wedding. Darren really enjoyed my dad, and the accident left both families reeling. We didn't think anything worse could happen, but soon we'd learn that more challenges were ahead.

A year after we were married, Darren noticed that one of his thighs was about two inches smaller than his other. He had kept himself in top physical form well after winning the Divisions III National wrestling championship years before. Testing finally revealed that he had inherited the gene for ALS (Amyotrophic Lateral Sclerosis), commonly known as Lou Gehrig's disease.

By the time Darren was diagnosed he had already lived longer than the average person with ALS. So began our panic. How would we live with this disease? Our marriage would not be long, and having children was no longer an option.

We had always wanted to move west. We did. To the county line. It was a beautiful piece of land with an old farm house, barn and pond. Darren thought this would bring him happiness. But after the first winter, we were both stressed. We had always wanted to travel. We did. In an RV. We spent a winter in Florida with people several decades older than us. It was interesting, but it didn't bring us happiness either.

Finally, we figured out that ALS was going to follow us wherever we went and whatever we did. Putting down roots seemed like a good idea. We planned to open a boarding kennel for dogs and cats on our country property. You don't get much more rooted than a boarding kennel. It's very demanding work.

Darren and I decided we needed to get serious about our faith. Going through this stressful time our own way was not working, and we were in despair. We attended church and Bible studies. We wanted answers. Or, at least some comfort.

While the kennel was under construction, we adopted Guinness, a 110 pound Newfoundland mix. I took him to obedience classes and he earned his CGC (Canine Good Citizen certificate). This is when I started to see the parallels between dog training and learning to follow God. I'd come home and report my observations to Darren. He'd share the profound thoughts he'd had while mowing the lawn. God was working in mysterious ways. We were just thankful He was at work.

In 1998, Good Shepherd Boarding Kennel was open for business. It was a good choice in that I stayed home and worked, while Darren was a substitute teacher. As he needed more help, I was there to provide it. The kennel forced me to get out of bed in the morning. And, I had to be nice to people. I didn't feel like doing either.

Strangely, being forced to function helped me and kept my attitude and stress in check.

Darren was an extrovert, and being around people was essential. It was truly his lifeblood, and he shined when he had an audience. He oozed charisma and won over nearly everyone he met. His attitude and bent sense of humor were contagious. People loved to be with him. When he substitute taught or helped with wrestling practices, all who met him were touched. Darren came home energized. We adopted Foster, a young Australian Cattle Dog who seemed to share Darren's sunny disposition.

In 1997, Darren's father showed signs of ALS and died within a year. Two years later, Darren's brother died from leukemia. People at the funeral home knew us by name.

ALS caused Darren's muscles to shrink on his bones. Our social life shrank as well. There was much we could not do and our isolation was difficult. We watched a lot of movies. We watched a lot of football. Mostly, we just watched life go on without us.

Foster and I shared a strong will, and going through dog obedience classes with him was completely different than with Guinness. Darren's illness progressed as had my contentious attitude toward God. Both Foster and I struggled, but we learned along the way.

Darren got beyond bitterness quickly and soon became passionate about his faith. God's comfort became real to him, and he realized that there was no hope beyond death without Jesus. All this I understood in my head, but my heart still resented that my life was going to go on beyond Darren's.

Darren died in July, 2003. Nearly eight hundred people attended his memorial service. After all our discussions and preparations for his inevitable death, it still was hard to believe he was gone. I spent little time thinking of what my life would be like without Darren. He said I probably would sleep the first year he was gone. He was right.

While the kennel and its routine was a comfort to me, I knew I couldn't do the work forever. As Darren figured out long before me, bitterness toward God was misguided. Instead, I experienced amazing comfort, well beyond what I imagined possible. As I tended the dogs in my care, I still thought of the metaphors of God's care for us.

While I stayed active with Bible studies, my friendship circle widened. After the encouragement of a friend, I began to write. As July 2004 approached, I dreaded my first wedding anniversary without Darren, to be followed by the anniversary of his death. A fictional story developed and absorbed me. This distraction made this time easier so I kept at it. By 2005, my energy level was restored and life with my friends was a joy.

Although missing Darren is a permanent part of me, I see the best parts of his personality alive and well in old and new friends. While I hadn't imagined what my life would be like in the post-Darren world, I certainly never thought it would be as good as it is.

So on that New Year's Day, 2006, I realized that after years of fighting God, I had finally learned to look to God for guidance and comfort. I had learned to heel right by His side and I wasn't going to leave Him. He had never left me. He had healed me.

SECTION ONE:
OBEDIENCE SCHOOL

You Belong to the Power You Choose to Obey

What is obedience? "To be willing to be guided" is one definition. Dogs need parameters of what's acceptable behavior and what is not. These are determined and taught by the dog owner. If the owner neglects this instruction, or is inconsistent, the dog is confused and usually follows his own rules, most of which are annoying to people.

Generally, dogs are happy to learn. They enjoy it. It's mentally challenging, and they like to understand how to please their owner. Apart from abuse and neglect, most dogs are devoted to their owner. They usually deem their owner trustworthy and reasonable, so they willingly choose to obey.

For people, following God is much more complicated. There's no leash leading to a visible person or "being." We don't get treats for all the good things we do, and we don't get whacked with a newspaper for the bad. (By the way, don't whack your dog with a newspaper – not a good training method). Trusting God is difficult. It can be so hard it has a word: faith.

Yet the principle is the same. We choose who or what to obey. If our greatest desire is acceptance by other people, we are guided by what others deem appropriate. If we want money or status, we follow the path we believe takes us there. Appetites drive others, whether physical hunger or sexual cravings. People have faith in these things bringing them pleasure, so they choose to obey these desires.

After much resistance, I've chosen to follow God. But the allure of the little gods (such as social status, sexual conquests) still entice me. I must remember their promise is hollow. Despite the short term gratification, they leave me wanting. We can fill ourselves with something less than Truth, but it will leave us hungry.

Each of us must make a choice, just like a dog does when choosing whom to obey.

Good = Boring?

Training isn't about having a better dog. It's about developing a dog that trusts its owner. Are trained dogs boring dogs? Some people just want their dog to be a "free spirit." "Well-trained" doesn't mean the dog has had all of its personality trained out, and anxiously awaits its next "order." Training does not create doggie robots. A well-trained dog is a happy dog, knowing its parameters. A happy dog knows its owner has its best interest in mind.

I have not been a perfect follower of Jesus. I have my stuff, but I've never felt my walk with God restricted my personality. A former roommate liked the fact that I could still follow Christ and still be a fan of the band Violent Femmes. She thought that was "cool." I think that's a compliment. And I take no credit for it – God made me the unique self that I am for His purpose, as He did each of us.

Being cool isn't important, but being one's own person is. I've met a lot of Christians who are oh so very "good," but seem miserable. If they have fun, they feel guilty. They are obsessed with being good – it becomes their god.

Following the rules isn't what God's Word really asks of us. God wants us to trust Him. When we trust Him, we see that His "rules" are for our own protection. He gives us parameters because He loves us and wants to protect us. Sin isn't bad because God randomly decided to make it so. Sin is bad for us. It has consequences – some that linger for years.

When we choose to do good for another, the action should flow from sincerity. When we get it backwards and do good deeds because we are obligated, that motivation may actually get in the way. It's easier to have all the externals – to look and do good – than it is to nurture a deep trust of God.

We may flail aimlessly without God, but with His parameters, we can flourish. That is what training is about. Not getting us to be better, but teaching us to trust God more. Good behavior is the outward appearance of that inward change.

SET UP FOR SUCCESS

Dogs often fail while they are learning. Just like a child, "no" is one of the first words they understand because they hear it all the time.

For this reason, they need to be successful at least part of the time during training. If the dog can sit for only three seconds, release the dog after two seconds and praise him. If the training session has been particularly difficult, finish with a command the dog can do easily and reliably. When training time ends with praise, the dog enjoys a sense of fun and accomplishment.

I prefer to avoid those things which I find difficult. But, every now and then, I'll try something new or difficult. Even if I can't do it well, I still learn in the process.

Contrary to what some think, following God is not about the "doing" as much as it is about the relationship. God isn't keeping track of my failures and achievements once I've entered a relationship with Him. Just as I would rather do something nice for a friend than embarrass them, I strive to do and be better to honor God and His love for me, not the other way around.

It is hard to know if Foster, my cattle dog, follows me from room to room because he likes me or because he wants something from me. And he pretty much embarrasses me all the time. But I love him because he's mine. It is a relief that I can count on God's forgiveness and faithfulness without condition.

> *"Therefore, since we have been justified through*
> *faith, we have peace with God through our Lord*
> *Jesus Christ, through whom we have gained access*
> *by faith into this grace in which we now stand.*
> *And we rejoice in the hope of the glory of God."*
> Romans 5:1-2

POLITICALLY CORRECT DOG TRAINING

The world of dog training has undergone a transformation - political correctness for the dog world. It began with the "all positive" approach to obedience training. That is, no negative consequences for undesirable behavior.

It's a beautiful theory...

I wish I could believe it worked in all circumstances. Not every technique works for every dog (or every dog owner). We learn differently. Personalities, families, environment, and experiences all shape how we take in information and process it.

Some dogs are naturally dominant. If they have been allowed to be completely unrestricted in their behavior, they are pretty wild and, if they are not food motivated, they really don't have any good reason to listen to a human and become "civilized."

The same may be said for people. If we are raised far from God, have had negative father-figure experiences and/or have every material need met, figuring out where God has a place in our lives is challenging.

We've all seen what happens to children when they aren't raised to believe the rules don't apply to them. No negative consequences make for a very unpleasant child (and resulting adult) who is hard to tolerate.

The world doesn't present us with many positive incentives. We learn differently. If a dog gets a collar correction, it will not suffer the rest of its life as a result of it. It may actually learn from it. Too many choices confuse dogs and people. Being collared by God's word keeps us protected from harmful consequences, as straying may cause far reaching problems.

A harsh come-uppance has been the best thing to happen to me, although I didn't think so at the time. In some instances, falling flat on my face has been the only way to true learning.

Fear Biter

A dog that has been abused or is a product of bad breeding will often be fearful. This is demonstrated by the dog cowering, growling, yelping, and sometimes screeching. It's generally unpleasant. Inadvertently, owners reinforce this behavior by cooing, "It's OK" and stroking the dog. This actually reinforces the fear in the dog and can make it worse. The behavior may even escalate to biting, given the right circumstances. Fear biters are tough to rehabilitate.

This dog lacks confidence. The dog may trust the owner and its immediate family in the secure comfort zone of its home. However, all other people, animals and environments are a threat.

Learning a variety of commands and being rewarded for good behavior and then successfully repeating the same commands outside the "security zone" is one step to build the confidence of the dog. Obedience classes are perfect for this dog as there are lots of new stimuli and the other dogs and owners know to give the dog time to learn.

People beaten down by life may be thought of as the human equivalent of a "fear biter." I can remember a time in my life when I thought I was in a safe environment, only to be hurt when most vulnerable.

It takes a while to rebuild confidence again. Some people give up. I found that when people disappointed me, God did not. He was the only true safe place. Even though it was hard to stay close to an Invisible God, He helped build my confidence again when I would come to Him. Unlike other times when I ran to Him with my problems, I was desperate this time. I didn't need a quick fix to the problem. I needed deep healing that wasn't going to come from people. God brought other wonderful people into my life to give me a "security zone" where I could build my confidence, and recognize that these kind people were the "God with skin on" I needed.

Once confidence is restored, the reflex "to bite first, ask questions later" disappears.

A Tired Dog is a Good Dog

Exercise is an essential part of a dog's life, especially puppies. Exercise is done through playing, chewing, and mental challenges. It is essential to the dog's well being. If a dog is confined for most of the day, its outlet of energy is usually seen in undesirable behavior like chewing the couch, tearing down the blinds, or even gnawing at their crate if they have nothing else to chew.

Many trainers suggest that the dogs be well-exercised before they come to obedience class. The dogs are less anxious and more focused for learning. If the dog has been crated all day and then let out when the owners come home and taken straight to obedience class, the dog is usually difficult to control.

On the other hand, if the dog enjoys a long walk with their owner and then goes to class, they can better focus. Trainers will also recommend not feeding the dog so the treats are more of a motivation.

Some people refer to the "exercise of prayer." Indeed, it is a discipline one has to do over and over until it becomes easier. It is not always convenient to "fit it in," but if

I actually enjoy what I'm doing (for me, several short prayers many times a day works best), it gives structure and focus to the day.

I realize that if I put prayer off until later in my day, when I've had breakfast and done the morning paper's sudoku puzzle, I'm not motivated to pray. If I start with prayer, I can focus better on my other tasks and generally feel more productive. By taking time out to think about what God wants me to do through the course of my day, the rest of my day is fully satisfying.

> *"For the eyes of the Lord range throughout the earth to strengthen those whose hearts are fully committed to him."*
> II Chronicles 16:9

CONTROL THE HEAD, CONTROL THE HEART

Trainers have raved over a relatively new training device called a head halter. It fits over the dog's head similar to a horse's halter and can cut training time in half. The principle is simple. When you control the dog's head, you control the rest of his body.

The dog can not drag the owner while out on a walk or lag behind. Jumping up on people or lunging at another dog is also controlled by the head halter.

I've recommended the head halter to many dog owners. Those who have utilized them are amazed that using such a small device results in big changes in the dog's behavior.

Similarly, the tongue is a small part of our human bodies. Our tongue also reveals who we are and in what direction we are headed. Ouch. I know – ouch! My words certainly can get me in trouble. Usually, it starts out innocently enough, but eventually the things I say I can not get back and I've headed down a bad path.

When I truly try to control the words that flow out of me, it's amazing how much better my little world becomes. No fear of gossip or profanity when I focus. I am more pleasant for others to be around. I even enjoy me more when I watch what I say.

I need a constant reminder that I need God's help to truly maintain control over my head and my heart.

> *"If anyone considers himself religious and yet does not keep a tight rein on his tongue, he deceives himself and his religion is worthless."*
> James 1:26

Attention, Please!

When I took Guinness, my Newfoundland mix, through obedience classes, the instructor called the very first exercise "getting their attention." The owner leashes the dog on a 20 foot lead and walks in a square pattern. The owner lets the dog do whatever it wants while the owner ignores the dog. The dog owner walks a straight line forward, about 15 feet. The dog usually bounds along and heads to the end of the rope, only to be brought up short. The owner then turns to the right, walks another 15 feet and stops. Same thing. Over and over, the dog runs to the end of the lead and has to stop at the end of the rope.

After a while, the dog usually figures out that if he doesn't want to get choked on the end of the leash, he had better keep his eye on his owner. The dog may think, "What is my owner doing? Where is s/he going? Maybe I should follow her/him so I don't get that nasty pain in my neck."

No harsh words are uttered by the owner, no words of consolation. The owner goes about his business of walking in a box. Guinness learned this pretty quickly and watched me before my next step.

How many times did I have to be brought up short before I learned to watch God? To trust Him to lead me? It took a long time. It's taken even longer to decide that I would actually follow once I figured out what He wanted.

God gives us a very, very long rope. Long enough to hang ourselves, one may say. However, He's always at the other end, and we can always turn and follow Him, realizing He knows what's best for us because He loves us. He lets us make our mistakes, and He waits for us to come back to Him. He longs for it.

> *"Jesus replied, 'You do not realize now what I*
> *am doing, but later you will understand.' "*
> John 13:7

ENOUGH ROPE TO
HANG OURSELVES

The leash used for the getting their attention exercise is no ordinary leash. The trainer usually suggests 12-20 feet, but anything more than 6 feet will work. Why the longer leash? Because if the dog is really rambunctious, he'll think he's free. He'll run full throttle until he discovers he's not free and gets a collar correction. (Remember, dogs have thick necks!)

The dog will bound and choose where it will go and what it will do. The owner may be ignored completely or followed closely. It may wander to their limit and then turn back to the owner.

So it is with God. He lets us go on for a very long time without us hitting the end of our rope. In fact, if we hit the end, we still don't have to turn around and follow Him. God won't drag us to the next corner of the square. He'll let us sputter and strain and do what we want for as long as we want.

The good news is, if we get to the end of that rope and realize we're in a bad place, we can turn around and see that God is there. He'll welcome us back.

I've found that God's word leashes me to goodness. While I can't see God, I have access to the words He gave for living my life with direction.

> *"Your word is a lamp unto my feet*
> *and a light for my path."*
> Psalm 119:105

A Gentle Correction

During obedience classes, I saw many young, energetic dogs bound to the end of their long leash, oblivious to their owner's whereabouts. They seemed genuinely surprised that they could not continue to proceed on their preferred path. When they turned to see what had happened, there was their owner, calmly moving in a different direction.

When we hit that end, who caused it? Who gently let us know we're at the end? If I had looked over my shoulder, God had been giving me a lot of hints that He might be able to help me with this little problem I was having. My little problem was, and often still is, "Doing it my way." He may not say anything when He turns a corner, and I'm too busy doing my own thing. I don't notice until I get to the end and feel my way going nowhere, hopeless.

Once I turn from my own stubborn ways, I can see that God's way is better, even if it wasn't my way.

A STIFF-NECKED PEOPLE

Why do dogs wear collars? Many dog owners are concerned that a collar is cruel. If collars are cruel, vets, humane society workers and dog trainers would let us know this. Usually, their own dogs wear collars.

The neck of a dog is not like our delicate little neck. "Ouch," we think. A dog's neck is very thick. They can wear a collar, and it serves a purpose, such as identification for the dog and a rabies tag.

Choke collars are controversial. For many years they've been used effectively, but for some trainers they've fallen out of favor. However, if used properly, they can be very effective. Despite the name, the purpose of the choke collar is not to choke the dog, but to get and keep attention quickly.

For really stubborn or strong dogs, pinch collars are another option. If you've ever seen one of them, they look like an instrument of torture. However, from personal experience with Foster, it was the only way I could communicate with him when he wanted to do his own thing. He was a very thick necked, strong-willed dog to train.

I always think of this when God called the Israelites a "stiff necked people." I think "thick necked people." It takes a lot to get through to me. I'm sure I needed the figurative pinch collar for any discipline to sink in to my being. Despite what it may have looked like on the outside, that moment of painful realization of being on the wrong path brought relief from greater harm.

"A man who remains stiff-necked after many rebukes will suddenly be destroyed – without remedy."
Proverbs 29:1

Alpha Dog Challenge

A major part of dog obedience is establishing authority. Communicating to the dog how it's in their best interest to willingly obey authority is what training is all about. In the absence of strong authority, a dog will fill the void with their own leadership. Generally, their house rules will be dramatically different from what you may have in mind.

Some breeds and some personalities tend to be more dominant, and strongly resist any other authority. These are commonly referred to as alpha dogs. While some trainers no longer ascribe to this notion, it seems to prove out when seeing Foster in action.

There is this phenomena that happens when an alpha dog gets challenged and loses their top dog position. They can get a little depressed. It happened with Foster during basic training.

While I don't think I'm nearly as pushy as Foster, I tend to resist orders. I like to get my own way. When I don't get my way, I pout. I get depressed. I withdraw. I find my prayers are more like a list of demands to push God into what I want. When I am busy pushing my own agenda, I rarely am able to look for God's work and His plan.

Often, when I really think about it, I usually can see that there was a better way than my own. While I still long to have control, following God's lead allows me to rest. Rest allows me to learn and see God's better way.

> *"My eyes are ever on the Lord, for only he*
> *will release my feet from the snare."*
> Psalm 25:15

Twenty Times a Day

The trainer leading our obedience class wanted us to practice the sit command with our dogs. Twenty times a day. Everyone was incredulous. "Twenty?! What about our day jobs?" Yes, twenty. She suggested we do five commands, four times a day. The dog had to sit to go out, sit to come in, sit to get a treat, get fed, play, etc.

The idea was to establish a pattern of the dog learning to listen to the owner. Learning to sit was secondary. The dog had to stop and think and look to the owner for what to do next. Once a dog is trained to sit regularly, he learns other commands more easily. He has established the habit of listening to his owner. The result is that the dog's attention and respect are focused on the owner.

I found this principle was true to my life with God. I needed to pray often and be mindful of God's place in my life. Or more to the point, my life and God's leading. To me, the practice of praying before meals is similar. It is another break in the day to focus on God and from where we receive our provision. When I stop and pay attention, I recognize that I have more awe and reverence for God, and at the same time, I love Him and desire to please Him.

> *"Your love, O Lord, reaches to the heavens, your faithfulness to the skies. How priceless is your unfailing love. Both high and low among men find refuge in the shadow of your wings."*
> Psalm 36: 5, 7

Say Please

Sit is probably the most common phrase a dog hears. Just why do we want our dogs to sit anyway? For one thing, this command is easy for a dog to learn. Once the dog learns to sit reliably, other commands are easier to teach. The dog has learned to listen to the owner and will soon learn new commands.

This command can be best used as a manner for the dog to "Say please." The dog has to earn everything – food, affection, trips outdoor, etc.

Foster is so good at learning to sit when he wants something that if I am walking past him with my dinner, he'll sit, run ahead of me, sit again, run ahead, sit….He's telling me he really wants what I've got. At least he's learned to tell me something.

When I remember to fit prayer time into my day, I like to pray on my knees. I didn't always, but once I started, I found that it felt really right for me. I felt like it was how to show God that I really was earnest.

The more I learned to go to God, the easier it became. Like so many things, it's a habit I needed to develop.

> *"For this reason I kneel before the Lord…to him who is able to do immeasurably more than all we ask or imagine, according to his power that is at work within us…"*
> Ephesians 3:14, 20

"Sit! Sit! Sit!"

Having a kennel, I see Dogs Gone Wild on many occasions. The owner gives a simple command repeatedly, "Sit! Sit! Sit! I said sit!" I watch in quiet amusement. The dog may or may not eventually decide to sit. These are situations where the dog is in full control of his owner.

Successful dog training requires teaching the dog to respond the first time a command is given. When told to "sit," the dog sits. During the initial training, of course, this is done with patience and the dog is gently put into the sit position. Once the dog understands, a treat is given. Command. Response. Reward.

Once the dog knows what is expected, the dog should respond immediately. And yes, in bigger dogs, sometimes it takes a little longer for the message in the brain to reach the tail end. So response times vary.

I think of the times when God has asked me to do something. I'd say my response time is a bit lacking. Sometimes, He gently puts me in the position I need to learn. But sometimes I ignore His call. He may even call me repeatedly, "Lynne, sit! Be still!" but I still do my own thing.

A dog that is not in control totally frustrates the owner. I'm sure I must frustrate God terribly by how willfully disobedient I can be. When I think about it, it's downright embarrassing. However, since His mercy and patience is boundless, He doesn't forsake me. On the other hand, He may decide to ask someone else to do what I ignored, and then I'm the one who's missed out on something great.

"Yet the Lord longs to be gracious to you; he rises to show you compassion. For the Lord is a God of justice. Blessed are all who wait for him!"
Isaiah 30:18

Leave It

Dogs really have no idea what is good for them and what is bad. It is as if they think, "I can do anything I want. Everything is OK." It's important for the owner to be discerning about what is in the dog's best interest, and to know how to communicate that to the dog.

"Leave it" instructs the dog to keep away from something that may be valuable to the owner or harmful to the dog. Obeying this command can quite literally mean life or death for the dog. If a stray animal like a raccoon comes on my property, I may instruct my dogs to "leave it" as it may fight with them, which could result in serious injury or illness for the dog (not to mention the raccoon). Also, if they decide to eat the days old trash they find on the road, they'll suffer (and so will I) from gastric problems.

Foster is a herding dog. He is driven by his instincts to chase things that move, which is most things in general. When he was a puppy, he particularly liked cars. I'd walk him on leash and he'd watch the cars go by. He didn't just notice them in passing, he hunched down when they approached, lunged as they got closer and turned around after they passed. When I saw him notice an approaching car, I'd tell him to "leave it." Now, he may notice a car, but doesn't try to hunt it down and kill it.

Foster still has an outlet for his herding though. He watches cars from the safety of the enclosed cab of my pick up truck. He will run the length of the cab trying to catch them. He especially likes big, noisy diesel trucks.

Foster may occasionally get frustrated by the limitations I put on him, thinking I allow him no fun. He doesn't understand that my rules are the result of my desire for him to be safe, healthy and happy.

Similarly, God provided us with the Ten Commandments. It's like the ultimate "leave it" list. We make choices, but there are consequences of things we've chosen to "ingest." His rules are not meant to spoil our fun, but to keep us safe, healthy and happy.

What You Can Have

Puppies are notorious for getting into trouble. While they are learning the rules of what's allowed and not allowed, pretty much everything goes in their mouths, including human hands and fingers. When people ask me how to keep their dog from biting, I tell them the best way is to always have something handy that the dog is allowed to have. That way, when the owner plays with his dog and the dog reaches for fingers or comes around the corner with something he can't have, the owner can give him a treat or toy he is allowed to have.

It is stressful for a dog to constantly hear "no," "drop it" and "leave it" and not know what is allowed. Reward good behavior. Once the permitted item is taken by the dog, be sure to acknowledge that he is "a good dog!"

Life isn't so simple that we are rewarded when we do the right things and punished when we do the wrong things. We can follow a narrow path and do all the right things and still have terrible things happen to us.

However, God does want us to understand that there are many wonderful things He created for us to enjoy. It is not difficult to see the beauty of God's creation. From complicated micro organisms to elaborate mountain ranges, every person can enjoy these obvious gifts. God offers even more than these visible gifts when we follow Him. There is deep abiding peace. There is guidance. There is security.

"For since the creation of the world God's invisible qualities – his eternal power and divine nature – have been clearly seen, being understood from what has been made, so that men are without excuse."
Romans 1:20

Halt!

For the most part, Foster is very good about sticking with me as I walk him. He wanders some but rarely runs so far ahead that I need to worry.

Foster, living by his motto of "what's next," tends to anticipate running to the truck when we get near the end of our walks. Near, to Foster, is about 300 feet. When we walk around home, he knows when we're within range of our return. But, there is a busy road to cross before we get there. If Foster is a little far, I call, "halt." He stops, and waits for the next command. He knows not to go any further.

This is a good command to stop a dog before s/he approaches something dangerous. If I'm walking Foster and I see another dog coming, I can yell "halt" and he'll stop. He looks at me and waits for my next command (usually, "ok" or "sit").

Sometimes God wants us to "halt" along the path we are traveling with Him. We don't always know the hazards that are ahead of us. He can see them clearly and knows the dangers. He wants us to stop where we are because we need to wait for Him to give us the next command. Do we wait before embarking on new ventures? Do we choose new paths without guidance? He knows the safe path for us.

> *"For I know the plans I have for you, declares the Lord, plans to prosper you and not to harm you, plans to give you hope and a future. Then you will call upon me and come and pray to me, and I will listen to you. You will seek me and find me when you seek me with all your heart."*
> Jeremiah 29:11-13

Drop It!

This command is different from the "Leave it" command. "Drop it" is used when the dog has forbidden fruit in his mouth. For obvious reasons, an owner has to be quick to give the dog this correction so that the object is not ingested.

So, whether it's something that must be handled with care like a child's new stuffed animal or a food item that will give your dog room-clearing gas for days, "drop it" is another essential command.

Foster is an opportunistic thief. If he can steal another dog's toy or bone, he'll do it. He'll sneak out of a kennel run and I can tell by his commando crawl that he has ill-gotten gain. "Drop it," I'll say, and he drops the plundered item.

I look back at times when I really, really wanted something. I can see how I had possession, or near possession, and couldn't wait to have it all to myself. But, then I saw it wasn't going to be the best for me. It may not have been mine to begin with. It may have caused me heart pain to ingest it. Bottom line, it wasn't good for me, even if I couldn't quite see it myself.

God wants us to drop all the things that keep us from a clear relationship with Him. Even if what we have looks delicious and we really want it, the long term effects are not good for us. God loves us enough to make it clear, if we'll only listen.

> *"For great is the Lord and most worthy of praise;*
> *he is to be feared above all gods. For all the gods*
> *of the nations are idols, but the Lord made the*
> *heavens. Splendor and majesty are before him;*
> *strength and glory are in his sanctuary."*
> Psalm 96:4-6

STAY

What's the difference between "halt" and "stay"? Halt is used when the dog is in motion and needs to stop. Stay is usually given when the dog is either standing, sitting or in a down position.

After halt, a dog waits for the next command. It is more of a pause (no, not paws). Stay is a command. Don't move until further notice is the message.

I know an owner who instructs his dog to go to its bed and tells him down and stay while eating a quiet meal free of begging and hot dog breath. What ambitious, organized owners! That must be the longest half hour of the drooling dog's life.

During training, a dog who gets up (usually to go to its owner, sometimes to sniff another dog) is given a quick "no" or correction and put right back into the stay position.

Many times I felt God had put me in a stay with no end in sight. For whatever reason, I needed to stay put, doing what I was doing. I didn't understand the purpose. I was perplexed, but I trusted there was a reason. This doesn't mean that I didn't try to get up and do something else, but I was usually put right back into the stay position.

Years later, I can see the wisdom of some of those situations. This builds trust for those times when God's wisdom is not as obvious to me.

"God is our refuge and strength, an ever-present help in trouble. Therefore we will not fear."
Psalm 46:1-2

"But we have this treasure in jars of clay to show that this all surpassing power is from God and not from us. We are hard pressed on every side, but not crushed; perplexed, but not in despair; persecuted, but not abandoned; struck down, but not destroyed."
II Corinthians 4:7-9

Time and Distance with Stay

When first teaching the stay command, the owner keeps the dog on a short leash and steps directly in front of the dog for about 10 seconds. The owner has the dog keep the position for short periods so it is not tempted to break position (either sitting or lying down).

As the dog learns to hold the stay position longer, the owner moves further away, eventually to the end of a 6 foot leash for several minutes. Dogs who train for the Canine Good Citizen test must be able to stay for a sustained 7 minutes without breaking. To add to the difficulty, the owner is out of the dog's sight.

As I've grown to know God and His ways a little better, I think God has used this principle with me. I hate staying when I don't know the purpose. However, I've seen that God has varied the amounts of time I've had to stay, and I've always known He was there, within sight.

Sometimes I can't understand the reason. Sometimes I feel like I can't see Him either. If it's God telling me what to do, then I slowly follow and trust the command, regardless of purpose.

I'll bet that good citizen certificate is in the mail.

"But those who hope in the Lord will renew their strength. They will soar on wings like eagles; they will run and not grow weary, they will walk and not be faint."
Isaiah 40:31

Wait

Stay and wait are two different commands. Wait is a temporary situation. Inevitably, whatever needs to happen next will come quickly. Stay is often used when the owner will be stepping away from the dog.

Foster needs the wait command often. He has my routine so figured out that he knows what is coming next and is eager to get to it. I need him to sit and wait while I open the tailgate of my truck. Otherwise, he's bouncing up and down and I can't get to the truck to open it. Other times I use it when we are walking side by side and I don't want him to dash ahead of me. Many times this is because of heavier traffic or a situation that may tempt him to act too quickly.

Foster probably dislikes the wait command more than most. For him, it is just putting off what is next for no good reason. I know the reason, but it's quite impossible to communicate the complexities to my dog.

Waiting on God. Be honest. How many times do we hear this? It's so very difficult. Waiting for me has seemed like years. I guess that's because it has been years. However,

I am not privy to God's plan behind all my waiting. Yes, there's the whole building character thing, and I guess that is important. But there are many complexities that I am sure I would not understand if God tried to explain His reasoning. And so, wait I must. I may get antsy, but it's better to wait on the Lord than race ahead and meet disaster.

A friend recently said, "Funny how just waiting and praying is such an active thing to do in God's eyes." I need to adjust my thinking. I do believe this is true. Doing nothing is harder for me than doing something. I can do very well. But I am not good at sitting on my hands, waiting. If I am prayerful and watching like Foster, I will become eager to follow through and do what God leads me to. Exercising my faith is movement in God's eyes.

SETTLE

Part of the appeal of puppies is their adorable wiggly-ness. They can hardly contain their excitement for people, food, toys, bones, leaves - just about everything. The hardest thing for puppies to learn is self-control.

The command settle is taught in puppy kindergarten classes. The owner gently places the pup on its side and tells it to settle. The goal is to have the pup lay still. Yes, it's a huge challenge. It is a gradual process of increasing how long the puppy will lie still. The goal is for the dog to lie quietly for about a minute. A very long minute.

In addition to self control, settle is useful for when the dog visits the vet as well as just getting the dog to be still for a while. Some trainers believe it establishes authority of the owner over the dog as well. It's generally one of the first training techniques taught.

Self control is a challenging concept to humans as well. We can be wiggly and get excited about everything that crosses our paths. "Be still and know that I am God" is difficult, particularly in our busy lives. Being still is hard enough. Trying to connect to God can be even harder.

But there is value in that quietness. Little by little, this is a valuable discipline to establish in our lives.

"Be still and know that I am God; I will be exalted among the nations, I will be exalted in the earth."
Psalm 46:10

No Bite!

Those tiny, needle-like puppy teeth! Ouch! Dogs learn a lot about their world by exploring it with their mouths. Puppies learn to interact with their litter mates by playing and biting. If they bite too hard, the other dog yelps and the play stops. If playing is desired, the pup learns to control biting. When the pups live with people, they have to learn the same boundaries.

Foster learned this one easily because he really wanted the play to continue. If he bit me or mouthed my hand too roughly, I'd respond with a high pitched "ouch" and I'd pull away my hand and stop playing. His reaction was to look at me. After a moment, play would resume. If he bit again, the play was stopped altogether.

God is unique because He is Holy. That's not a word that is heard often, and it's hard to define. He loves us. He sent us Jesus to show that love. He wants a close relationship with us. But, we are not equal with God. He lets us know a lot about Himself through the Bible, but we don't know everything. It wouldn't make sense to us, for one thing. However, the idea here is that we can't roll around and play bite with God like He is our equal. He wants us to enjoy life, enjoy Him, but we need to respect who He is. He is our Provider and our Protector. Yet, He is still Holy, All-powerful, and All-knowing.

"There is no one holy like the Lord; there is no one besides you; there is no Rock like our God."
I Samuel 2:2

Perfect Obedience

When a dog becomes confused during training, it will likely communicate this by lying down. The dog doesn't understand the owner. It becomes immobile. Rather than risk displeasing the owner, the dog does nothing.

It would be better for the dog to attempt to follow rather than do nothing. Then the dog would be told "no" and the owner has the opportunity to put the dog into the correct position for the command. The key is for the owner to show the dog the correct position and not act like the misstep is a big deal. A mistake was made. It's time to move on.

Mistakes are often part of learning. According to this logic, I should be a genius. I am not, in spite of many mistakes throughout my life. In fact, I continue to get things wrong. However, I try to no longer dwell too much on the missteps. I try to figure out what I did wrong, and then move on.

Making mistakes makes us vulnerable to the pain of failure. This pain is real. Like all people, I've experienced hurtful situations and broken relationships. I am not eager to repeat that pain. Whether it was my fault, the other person's or some combination, it makes one cautious about future relationships.

However, the alternative is to do nothing and be isolated. It takes courage to take another risk. Even with the very real possibility of future mistakes, I'd rather suffer those and learn something in the process than be paralyzed with fear.

God's forgiveness through Jesus' atonement is just the badge of courage I need to take risks. If I do mess up (and I will), I can seek God's promise of forgiveness. If I am hurt by another, God is there to strengthen me. This true liberation helps me move forward in life.

Waving the White Flag

Some dogs come to obedience classes a little older than others. They are used to doing things their own way and ignoring the owner. Training classes shift authority, and this dog may dig in, refusing to change its ways. The owner must determine to be patient with the dog as it makes its mistakes and resists.

The owner's goal should be to get the dog to obey willingly and happily. After a dog gives up his position of control, he often will cling to the owner for comfort and show his trust.

Happily? Maybe not. Sure, we all want to be in control. I know I do. I need to constantly remind myself that I am not. I'm not qualified to make all the decisions in the universe the way God can. That whole all-knowing, all-powerful aspect of God makes Him qualified. There's a certain amount of peace in that. Going to God for His love and in to His trusting, knowing arms is much easier once I realize that His ways are not mine. They are better.

Obstacle Course

Classes that incorporate obstacle courses in their training help fearful dogs build confidence. It mentally challenges confident dogs as well. Most obstacle courses include ramps, jumps and tunnels. First, the dog has to be shown how to maneuver these obstacles. It takes many "do-overs" before the dog gets the idea. But, to get through the course, mastering each obstacle is essential.

Nearly every dog that successfully goes through an obstacle course is thrilled to have accomplished this feat. My very shy dog, Guinness, used to come off the final ramp with tail held high, wagging at the applause he received. It built the bond between us as well.

It's an understatement to say that life brings us challenges. Often, they get harder before they get easier, if they get easier. Some people shy away from the challenges and some won't even venture onto the course. For those who tackle a challenge, a sense of accomplishment awaits.

Life with my husband had many challenges that both of us had to maneuver. We didn't want to, but we had no choice. While we weren't pleased to be on a difficult course, we eventually figured out if we wanted to get through it, we'd have to look to our guide. God had put people into our lives who had their own hard times. Their support was invaluable. Our trust in God deepened, so that when faced with the next hurdle, we knew what to do.

Finishing pretty isn't what counts, it's finishing. If you can wag your tail at the end, that's just bonus.

> *"Let us throw off everything that hinders and*
> *the sin that so easily entangles, and let us run*
> *with perseverance the race marked out for us."*
> Hebrews 12:1

The Tunnel

The most difficult obstacle for a dog to master is the tunnel. Going through that narrow space for a distance is intimidating. Some courses have a blind tunnel in which the dog cannot see the end. This is really tough. A dog must trust their owner to lead them all the way through to safety. This is a major bond-building obstacle.

The tunnels people face are just as daunting. How long is this tunnel? How can I get through? What is on the other side? Will more challenges await me there?

If we don't trust who takes us through a tunnel, it is that much worse. We may back out or we may be drug through anyway.

One of my friends who was key in my own crisis told me at one point, "I feel like I am emerging from this dark tunnel, and I am reaching back to you to pull you through." That picture has stayed with me a long time. I so needed her pulling me as her journey, her success eased my own.

Now, I find myself reaching for others who are in the middle of a tunnel. Some have backed out. That is understandable. However, to stay on course is to achieve with God what doesn't seem possible when you face the darkness. Coming through on the other side with God's help builds our bond with Him.

"You, O Lord, keep my lamp burning; my
God turns my darkness into light. With
your help I can advance against a troop;
with my God I can scale a wall."
Psalm 18:28-29

THE RAMP

Obstacle courses have ramps of varying sizes that dogs run up and down. At each end of the ramps the base is shaded. The dog must step on this shaded area. This way there is no unfair advantage for a dog to leap midway up the ramp, dash over the top, and then leap back to the ground. Failure to hit this mark results in "points off" the dog's score. This is a rigid but respectable rule for dog competitions.

At one point, I worshipped in a legalistic religious environment. An individual's choice of what to watch on television (or not), and appropriate music, and political views were all subject to strict "rules."

Since I was at a point of growing spiritually, this strictness had some appeal. Both my husband and I suddenly rethought all of our behaviors. In some instances, this was a good thing. However, this narrow thinking crept into obsession and micro-managing every aspect of our lives. I got really good at applying this strict thinking to not just myself but to others as well. As a result, we both became miserable. There was no joy in following the Lord. The idea of a relationship was replaced by rules.

"I desire mercy, not sacrifice." This was a startling verse when I read it. God wants me to be kind, as opposed to strict? Wow, that was radical. When my husband and I finally understood the concept of "grace," our joy returned. Now following the Lord was a joy. He wanted us to live a life pleasing to Him, but not obsessing on every detail. Allowing God's quiet spirit to shape us was a much better way to live.

> *"For I desire mercy, not sacrifice,*
> *and acknowledgement of God*
> *rather than burnt offerings."*
> Hosea 6:6

Casual Obedience

There are a lot of dogs out there that have never been "to school." They've not been trained by a diligent owner. Or, perhaps they have been trained, but the owner doesn't reinforce the commands at home. The dog really picks and chooses when he is going to obey the owner, and when he's going to "do his own thing." The dog obeys when it's convenient and easy to do so. One of the dangers is that the dog won't obey when it's important or even in a life-threatening situation. Obedience is important.

My walk with God had a very long period of casual obedience. Even though I had a decent understanding of what God wanted from me, I would select what I wanted to do and ignored God's larger plan. However, when a threatening situation was upon me, I didn't know what to do. I would wonder what was going on. I thought, "how did this happen?"

I shouldn't have been taken by surprise. I had taken God far less seriously than I should have. It's taken me years to readjust my thinking to see that God's ways are indeed better than my ways. Basically, I didn't want to grow up. More accurately, I thought I was grown up and was "done." God doesn't show us all our mistakes at once (thank you). It's normal for a puppy to chew the couch when it's young, but is far from understandable when it has grown.

Mistakes are always part of our lives, but now my mistakes are generally not as big as they were before I walked God's narrow path. In many ways, I've grown beyond puppy kindergarten.

> *"Though by this time you ought to be teachers, you need some one to teach you the elementary truths of God's word all over again. You need milk, not solid food! But solid food is for the mature, who by constant use have trained themselves to distinguish good from evil."*
> Hebrews 5:12, 14

OBEDIENCE IS THE EVIDENCE OF CHANGE

One thing constantly amazes me about obedience training. It works! I know that's pretty obvious, but there are always those dog owners who are reluctant to put the effort and money into teaching their dog basic skills.

But even a little obedience makes a difference. When a friend asked me about her dog's sudden willful disobedience, I gave her a quick tip. Try twenty sits a day. She was amazed at what a big difference that made in the dog's overall behavior.

Obviously, training a dog from a young age is ideal. I've suggested to many dog owners that if they do no other training, invest in puppy kindergarten. It's much easier to develop good habits and keep them going than it is to undo bad behavior.

The same has been true of me. When I finally began to pay attention to God, my changes were gradual. I had a lifetime of bad habits to change. But simply making the effort to pray on a daily or semi-daily basis brought me closer to God immediately. It doesn't always work that way, but it made a difference for me and others noticed a difference too. It seemed kindness wasn't so difficult. Being patient and more forgiving was a joy, not a burden or duty.

I wanted to do more. I learned a little. I wanted to learn more.

"And I pray that you, being rooted and established in love, may have power, together with all the saints, to grasp how wide and long and high and deep is the love of Christ."
Ephesians 3:17

Life Long Instruction

Guinness wasn't exactly a quick learn, but he tried pretty hard and enjoyed both training classes and sessions at home. Sit was added to his vocabulary easily, even though it seemed to take a long time for the message to leave his brain, travel his long, Newfie body and put his tail to the ground.

I was pleased that he knew sit. But, when the opportunity arose, he would still chase the cats and pull at his leash during walks. I was pleased, but I wasn't satisfied. He had a long way to go.

He continued to improve, and once he learned leave it, the cats were safe. Instructors will remind you that training doesn't end when classes are over. It's life long. Basic manners are established, but improvements and adjustments are necessary for the lifetime of the dog.

I recently heard it said that pleasing God is easy, but satisfying Him is impossible, until we restore our lives through His Son, Jesus.

That seems reasonable. We do please Him easily. We share our toys, we smile at each other and we resist the urge to chase after things we aren't supposed to have.

But, is He satisfied with us? Are we satisfied with ourselves? Are we satisfied with others? No, we have a long way to go. Others disappoint us. We disappoint ourselves.

We break the rules. We can't live up to them. We may continue throughout our lives to improve and learn more. Yet we still experience disappointment. We know what perfection is. We've been given the idea in our heads for a reason. No one attains perfection.

Reconciliation is possible. One perfect sacrifice made us acceptable to God. Because of Jesus, we can fully satisfy God.

> *"Without faith, it is impossible to please*
> *God, because anyone who comes to him*
> *must believe that he exists and that he*
> *rewards those who earnestly seek him."*
> Hebrews 11:6

SECTION TWO:
THE DINGO

INDEPENDENT THINKER

Foster is a cattle dog, which means he was bred to organize a herd of testy bulls and sloth-like cows into an assigned area. Cattle dogs get kicked in the head and seem not to notice as they continue their work. They figure out their task by sizing up the situation, without much help from the owner. It's an incredible instinct.

Foster has no cattle to herd, just my cats. He's taken it upon himself to enforce rules I never made. He's made his own decisions on their conduct. I must say he's made some good choices.

Herding breeds tend to be independent thinkers. They generally need a really good reason to give up their system of doing things for their owner. They are stubborn, not because they are lazy, but because they won't go along with just any system.

Following God is extra hard when you possess good decision making skills and reasoning abilities. I have had an attitude of "I've done pretty well myself. Why should I go along with this?"

However, I am not perfect. No, really. Like everyone, I have made my share of mistakes. (It hurt to write that, but it's true.)

Trusting God with His system has been difficult, but I see His wisdom in some things. In the things where I can not see His wisdom at work, I've had to learn to trust that He is in fact making good decisions. Often when I have no possible solution, God, in His incredible timing, provides an answer.

> *"But he knows the way that I take; when he has tested me, I will come forth as gold."*
> Job 23:10

Alpha Complex

My dog is a bully. It's embarrassing. I have to watch him around other dogs so he doesn't tangle with them. While most dogs happily play and frolic, Foster gets bent out of shape if he is inappropriately sniffed. At first, he will only raise his hackles and look at the offending dog sideways. If the dog doesn't back off, he snaps his Cayman-alligator jaws at him. Then, the other dog backs off. However, Foster occasionally gets into a fight and it's really awful for the ten seconds it usually lasts.

Some dogs are genuine leaders and don't like to play by rules other than their own. They are hard to train because they are quite intelligent. This is different from dogs that are people pleasers. They are easy to train because they just want a pat on the head and your happy voice as their reward. Not so with the alpha dog. He needs a good reason to obey.

I have been known to be, on occasion, a bit, well, difficult. I once asked my husband if he thought I was stubborn and he laughed for ten minutes straight. But I digress. While I know perfectly well how to behave in groups when I'm not in total control, there is that part of me that wonders why the leader gets to tell me what to do. In other words, "Why should I listen to you?"

As one might imagine, this makes following an unseen God a little difficult for me. I do, however, respect Him. So, being All-Powerful, All-Knowing, All That Stuff, I do believe He knows a few things about the operation of the universe. However, I do tend to question why He asks me to follow Him and do things I don't fully understand. Frankly, I occasionally raise my hackles. "What are you doing to me, God? Are you sure?"

My little alpha complex really can't get me anywhere worth going. The Alpha and Omega, He is worth following, even when I question authority.

WHAT ARE WE DOING NEXT?

Foster loves to go places. When I put down the tailgate of my pick up truck, he jumps in enthusiastically and does the most obnoxious hopping you can imagine. Friends think it's cute until drool pours from his mouth in anticipation of his big adventure.

Foster doesn't care where we are going, as long as we go. Being in motion is all he cares about. If I am driving on a busy road, he stands at the front of the enclosed cab, looking out the window. When he sees a truck approach from the opposite direction, he goes to the side. As the truck passes, he leaps and runs the length of the truck, barking at it. He'll do this for miles. It's quite a sight.

Foster's motto is "not what we're doing now, but what we're doing next." When returning from a walk, Foster's demeanor changes when we get within sight of our truck. It doesn't matter that we have a quarter mile to go on our walk. All he can think about is going to that truck. It always bugs me that he isn't enjoying the last part of the walk because he's fixated on going to that truck.

We, too, miss the journey of our lives if we look too far down the road at what might be next. There is plenty to occupy us on the way - so much to enjoy. We will become anxious if all we can think about is the future.

God says, "I know the plans I have for you." Since He knows and isn't telling, we can strive to trust His plan and be less anxious.

> *"Peace I leave with you, my peace I give you. I do not give to you as the world gives. Do not let your hearts be troubled and do not be afraid."*
> John 14:27

Leaving What's Good
for What's Better

One morning, I was walking Foster down a country road. Not being a high traffic area, I let him off his leash to run and sniff at will, while I kept a close eye on him.

I passed him as he was wolfing down a treasure of some stale chips found by the side of the road. I wondered what kind of effect this might have on his stomach. Continuing at my pace, I looked back and noticed he was still with the bag, but a look of confusion came over him. I had moved beyond his normal comfort zone distance. He looked again at the bag and then at me. With one more glance at the chips, he sprinted to catch up with me.

So often I have the same problem trying to decide if I want to give up the lousy stale chips I am tempted to choose over God. I can either settle for fulfilling a craving I have immediately, or I can look to a higher, more permanent good. God desires to give us good food, good things. Yet, I may only see what I have in front of me at the time, not even recognizing that these crumbs are not good for me.

Foster receives much more than just his next meal from me. I am his sense of security, his outlet for fun and exercise, as well as his shelter from the elements. I need to remember that God provides for me in many of these same ways.

"Command those who are rich in this present world not to be arrogant nor to put their hope in wealth, which is so uncertain, but to put their hope in God, who richly provides us with everything for our enjoyment."
I Timothy 6:17

Pay Off vs. Consequences

Foster, like all dogs, follows a pretty simple philosophy. Is the pay off I receive from this behavior greater than any consequence I may incur? For instance, stealing a juicy burger off a plate at a picnic is usually well worth the scolding. If he is successful at it once, chances are good he'll try it again. If chasing the cat around the house isn't worth 15 minutes of time out confinement, then Foster may choose to ignore that tantalizing feline.

It seems like I follow this philosophy too. Is eating a piece (or more) of this triple layer chocolate cake worth the extra aerobic workout (or more) I'll need?   Is not returning the phone call of a long winded but lonely person worth the guilt?

Is following God worth it or not? Do I really need to listen to Him? What's the payoff? Some may think it's a simple answer of "Heaven or Hell." There's a lot more to it, really. A friend of mine puts it like this, "It's possible to live without God, but it sure ain't pretty." It's true, God lets us live apart from Him. He loves us enough to let us come to Him freely, not as a tyrannical lover.

We get to choose. After testing His ways, His character, His Word, I have learned that living with God is much easier than without. I can't fully comprehend God's power, peace and love. But, He is very worth serving and having in my life.

> *"Find rest, O my soul, in God alone; my hope comes from him. He alone is my rock and my salvation; he is my fortress, I will not be shaken. My salvation and my honor depend on God; he is my mighty rock, my refuge."*
> Psalm 62:5-7

No Begging

When I was a kid, our dog, Brandy, begged for scraps when we were having our family meals. As the dog only sat by one person, we knew the culprit was Dad. My husband carried on this tradition in our home. I remember several times Foster and Guinness and a couple cats hovered around him while he tried to eat. I ate my meal in peace, animal free.

Trainers tell owners that feeding the dog table scraps is a major no-no. Dietary concerns are one reason. Dog food has been specially formulated to be nutritionally complete with sufficient fat and calories for dogs. Anything additional is extra fat and calories, which makes the dog gain weight. I've often wished I ate kibble so I didn't get off track with my diet.

The second reason to refrain from feeding table scraps to a dog is because it does make them a terrible beggar. In effect, they become a slave to begging. When they could be playing or going outside, they are preoccupied with the idea that there is food in the room. They must wait for a chance to get it. Foster has forgone a good game of Frisbee because someone had a bag of chips open. It was all he could think about until they were out of sight and scent.

I can think of a time or two when I focused on what was unhealthy for me rather than engaging in healthier behaviors. Feeding my appetites can become a powerful master that I feel compelled to serve. Self-control is hard.

If I put my relationship with God first, I notice that this is a more satisfying replacement for the lesser desires and appetites I pursue.

Break Down

Traveling back from Chicago one day, my car's transmission gave its last gasp. It actually sounded more like a scream. I was stranded. It came at a most inopportune time. I was struggling with some changes and pleading with God to bring good things into my life. And then the engine gave. Not exactly the answer I was looking for at the time.

However, as I waited (2.5 hours) for the tow truck, I wasn't angry. I was thankful it was not raining, I was not in immediate need of restroom facilities, and it was still daylight. I had my dog with me, which made me feel protected (particularly later while riding with the scary tow truck driver). When I started my trip, I threw my Bible in the car at the last minute. That was my only reading material while I waited.

I wasn't spared the tough experience of my car breaking down. There, at the side of the road, God was with me. It was also so with the situation in which I was wrestling with God. I wasn't going to get out of this uncomfortable situation, but I knew He would be there to go through it with me.

*"Show me your ways, O Lord, teach me your paths;
guide me in your truth and teach me for you are God
my Savior, and my hope is in you all day long."*
Psalm 25:4-5

Getting Too Comfortable

Foster has gotten too comfortable in his obedience. He thinks he knows the rules, so why listen to me? He takes his time responding to my commands. This does not please me.

Trainers recommend going back to basics when a dog gets sluggish with his obedience. The owners need to go back to the twenty sits a day to reinforce who is in charge. Also, have the dog heel on walks.

It's a good reminder. I get sluggish with my faith walk. I know the rules, so I don't need to hurry to follow what God might be saying. He might be saying, "I mean now" as I often do with Foster. If I can remember how impatient I get with Foster, maybe I'd pay more attention and make a quick response to God's leading.

I need to get back to basics when I get sluggish with my faith. Read my Bible more frequently – remind myself that He's in charge. And to follow closely at His heels, so I don't miss where God is leading.

Enforcing the Rules

Foster's nickname (besides "The Dingo") is the Enforcer. He doesn't like the cats jumping on the table or bed. He doesn't like it when I give them a treat. In Foster's mind, this is breaking the rules since he can't do those things. However, I allow the cats to do these things and have these privileges.

I once was a great enforcer of what I thought God's rules were. It bugged me when others weren't following the rules as I saw them. I couldn't understand why others would watch certain television shows or go to certain places.

Then, I learned that I can't follow the rules either. I learned about God's grace. And that was a gift. God has more grace than I can imagine. He is forgiving and kind. While I don't understand all, I do see how beneficial God's grace is to me. For this reason, I must extend this grace to others.

SNACK TIME!

One of my kennel clients always brings Foster a snack when she comes to pick up her dog. Sometimes I get one too. Both of us are pretty happy to see her. When she pulls into the driveway, Foster can barely contain himself. He circles and hops until I open the house door. Then he runs as fast as he can towards her. It looks like he'll run right into her at top speed. Somehow, he screeches to a stop and sits eagerly at her feet, awaiting his treat. Inevitably, he's rewarded with a crunchy treat, which he gobbles up immediately. Then he looks for more. Ingrate.

There are few things in life that draw that level of enthusiasm from me. Yet, there should be. God has given me so many good things, yet I can act indifferently toward them. What would my life be without Jesus? I can't imagine my life without the deep peace and assurance He offers for our walk through life. And forgiveness, love, and direction – what would I do without His influence?

My problem is when I can't see something in front of my nose, I tend to miss it. Or, I just plain forget. If God would pull into the driveway with a big box of His gifts, I'm sure that would generate sincere excitement on my part. Instead, I need to discipline myself daily. I'm not saying I do. I'm saying I need to. By spending time in prayer and studying God's word, I am constantly reminded of much goodness available from the Lord. And the reward is longer lasting than a dog biscuit. And I am grateful.

> *"O Lord you are my God; I will exalt you and praise your name, for in perfect faithfulness you have done marvelous things, things planned long ago…He will swallow up death forever. The Sovereign Lord will wipe away the tears from all faces."*
> Psalm 25: 1, 8

SECTION THREE:
KENNEL DOGS

WHOSE WE ARE

"My dog's very well behaved." I've heard that more than a few times on the phone when an owner is making a reservation for their dog to stay at my kennel. I don't expect dogs to be well behaved at the kennel. It's kind of like camp and they get to do things they don't always get to do at home. I know when I'm not in there, the dogs are staying up late and talking about boys (and girls). The popcorn kernels I find the next morning pretty much give them away.

When some of these alleged well behaved dogs arrive, they are dragging the owner around the car, lunging at me, putting their paws on my shoulders and barking excitedly. Like I said, I'm ok with this. But what was the owner thinking? This is not a well-behaved, controlled dog! A well trained dog behaves consistently, despite circumstances.

Christians are cited as being horrible hypocrites. One person explained that a sinner realizes they are continuing to sin, but realize that it is, in fact, sin. A hypocrite, however, sees no conflict between their sinful behavior and condemning others.

Christians make mistakes and sin. Sometimes they are big ones that make others wonder who we belong to. If I say I am a follower of Christ, I had better act like it, even if no one is watching.

It's something each of us has to work on daily. Act like you belong to someone you care about. Someone you don't want to misrepresent.

Those of us who follow God still mess up. But we rely on our Lord's forgiveness. Those who don't follow God and mess up aren't really hypocrites as they don't claim to belong to anyone but themselves. And they just don't know what they're missing.

> *"I do those things I do not wish to do and*
> *don't do those that I wish to do."*
> Romans 7:15

Essential Socialization

When my husband came up with the name for our kennel, Good Shepherd, I didn't think beyond the similarity of dog breed and attribute of God. Once I began my role as kennel operator, I realized just how similar my role is to a shepherd.

Herding dogs outside several times a day and back into their kennel is a lot of work. Sometimes, I have small play groups that go out together. When they come back in from their play time, they normally go straight to their run, lapping up water and gobbling their food. Dogs less social sometimes are uncooperative when going back into their runs. They are more likely to be poor eaters.

The dogs who expend energy and are stimulated mentally by their time with other dogs are happy boarders. They are eager to go out and play again. They are also more content within their own runs and rest well.

Church is hard for me. Worship is meaningful, but the social dynamics can be complicated and difficult. Yet, it is clear from God's Word that we are to meet together, strive with one another, and pray for each other. God must have good reason to emphasize this point repeatedly.

In all communities of believers, there are times of stress when people don't get along. There have been many times when a couple dogs will suddenly go from playing to fighting, and I have to break it up. At my kennel, I solve disputes. In a church setting, I find myself often being that person who takes issue with someone. As I get older, I am learning better how to handle conflicts.

Whether it is a formal church or an informal Bible study, I have learned that meeting together is important. Even when it is difficult and uncomfortable, I find being together through loving God is healthy. I spend a lot of time by myself. Thankfully, I'm very comfortable keeping my own company. In fact, it would be easier to do so. I must remind myself that complacency is not what God is about. Instead, He wants to see me risking and learning. I don't push myself because "God says so," but because it is worth doing.

The Sound of Your Voice

I do not let sleeping dogs lie. When I go out to the kennel first thing in the morning, it's quiet until the door opens. Then, the barking begins. Dogs have different barks for different things. When that door opens, most sound an alarm bark – the deep, husky, menacing tone that warns the intruder off. However, when I greet them with "good morning dogs," the barks change to excited ones that anticipate positive activity.

Seeing the inside of a boarding kennel is kind of like watching sausage being made – you don't want to see it, just trust the process. It ain't pretty. When a dog owner is visiting for the first time, I let them see the inside kennel runs, the outside respite areas, and the play room. I explain a typical day's care for each dog and other details.

One thing that I tell them is that once they come to pick up and drop off their dog, it's preferable for the owner to wait outside. When people other than me enter the kennel, the dogs again use their warning bark and dogs that are normally complacent can become agitated. The dogs are already under stress from being away from home.

If the owner can wait outside, it will make life easier on all the dogs.

I'm surprised at how quickly most dogs accept my authority as temporary caretaker and respond to my voice without alarm. Hearing the tone of the barks change with a simple greeting is gratifying.

The Lord has said, "My sheep know my voice." I honestly never understood this until I saw it demonstrated with the dogs. If we truly belong to God and trust Him, we can rest at ease in His care. There are many other voices that call to us – just look at television advertising! The temptation to give into mass consumerism and acquiring more and more stuff is indeed everywhere. But what does God call us to do? He wants us to serve others, not ourselves. He wants us to give of ourselves in both resources and time.

The more we study what God gave us through the Bible, the more familiar we are with His message. Then, when we walk through our every day lives, His voice can be heard. We know the peace that passes all understanding.

"Whether you turn to the right or to the left, your ears will hear a voice behind you, saying, 'this is the way; walk in it.'"
Isaiah 30:21

"He calls his own sheep by name and leads them out. When he has brought out all his own, he goes on ahead of them, and his sheep follow him because they know his voice."
John 10:3-4

"Today, if you hear his voice, do not harden your hearts."
Hebrews 3:7-8

Psycho-Freak Dogs

Part of my job as kennel owner is to love the dogs in my care. This usually manifests itself in kind words, pats on the head, and a lot of patience. No wonder the Bible stresses patience so much. It may be specifically for kennel keepers. The only jobs I know of that require more patience are groomers, and even more so, mothers.

For 99.9% of the dogs I've watched over the years (somewhere around 500), liking the dogs is easy. Yes, some are willful, some are exuberant, but they are at the kennel, and I don't expect them to be on their canine good citizen behavior. They generally act like dogs. I don't mind the spilled water bowls, the jumping up and muddied clothes.

On rare occasion, I kennel the type of dog I kindly refer to as the psycho-freak dog. These dogs (of which there are thankfully few) are completely undisciplined. Consistently, their owners have no control at home. They don't seem to be able to establish any authority over their dog.

However, my job is still to care for these dogs. Feeding them, cleaning up after them is easy compared to saying nice things and petting the psycho-freak dog. But I still have to do it. Even though it's beyond me, the owners still love their unruly dog.

These dogs were not taught basic manners. They barely know English. How can I expect them to understand when they've not been taught? When I told a friend that I'm required to be nice to them anyway, she said, "Especially be nice to them." Ouch.

You've met the human equivalent of the psycho-freak dog, I know you have. They drive you completely nuts. They are severely lacking in some area. Their behavior is beyond comprehension. How can anyone stand these people? It's easy to be kind to nice, normal people. The test is being kind to the difficult people each of us has in our lives.

God loves these people. And He loves us too, despite our own psycho-freakness.

Obsessive Obedience

When an owner picks their dog up from the kennel, it is generally a happy, exuberant reunion. The dog will jump up and bark - general mayhem. I've seen many a male owner wish he'd worn protective coverings.

For one of the dogs I watch, that natural enthusiasm is squashed by an owner who expects constant, perfect obedience. When it's time for the dog to go home, the dog is ordered to come, sit, and get in the car. The dog can't jump or run like he wants to. The owner doesn't even touch the dog. It kind of breaks my heart.

Obedience gives us good parameters for behavior, but it's not supposed to be a burden for the dog or the owner. Training is supposed to be fun, and it really builds bonds of love and trust between dog and owner. By knowing the rules, the dog understands what's expected and how best to please his owner.

Becoming a slave to perfect obedience to God kills our joy. At one point in my spiritual journey, I was obsessed with perfect obedience. I was miserable. This isn't what God wants. Jesus said that He takes our yokes so that "our burdens are made light." Following God is supposed to be joyful, even exuberant. Sometimes I think that when I see God face to face, I'll run up to him, tail wagging, and lick His face. So to speak.

Obedience liberates us to love God freely.

"Come to me, all you who are weary and burdened, and I will give you rest. Take my yoke upon you and learn from me, for I am gentle and humble in heart, and you will find rest for your souls. For my yoke is easy and my burden is light."
Matthew 11:28-29

GAINFULLY EMPLOYED

Each purebred dog is bred deliberately to perform a specific task. Even dogs bred specifically for companionship have deliberate physical and mental traits. A retriever wants to bring back the duck. A herding breed wants to keep the group together by rounding them up. A pointer marks game for the hunter.

When dogs don't have an outlet for what they are naturally born to do (long walks, Frisbee, etc.), they get into trouble. A key training adage is "a tired dog is a good dog."

Certainly it's true with people as well. When we are bored, we tend to get into trouble. We need to find the best place to use our talents. Ideally, we use them not just to serve our own needs, but also to serve the needs of others.

Dogs were bred to serve man's needs. Perhaps this is a good model for us to serve others and to serve God. It is what we were born for.

Elvis has Left the Building

Elvis has been coming to the kennel for several years. I love Elvis. He's the smartest Border collie I've ever watched. His instinct to herd is like no other. When dogs run amok, Elvis lends a helping paw to get them back into their kennel runs. He stares at them with his steely eyes and directs them right where they need to be. He is better at this job than I am.

I asked the owner if Elvis ever herded up their kids. They said he's never done any herding at home. He's a city dog. When Elvis sees dogs hopping up excitedly on their back legs at the kennel, he does not like this lack of decorum. Something in his doggie brain kicks in. Basic training goes out the window. He won't go back to his own cage or relieve himself if he's distracted by herding duty.

I have a few vices. Only a few – really. Most of the time, I keep them in check. Most of the time. Other times my best notions of moderation are abandoned and my instinct to keep going takes over. Of course, basic obedience or self-control went out the window (sometimes me with it).

Our instincts to sin can take over quickly and easily. As rational human beings who can exercise will power, we need to reign in our worst instincts to enjoy the good things in life. Sometimes we need a little help from our friends. All the time, I need God's power to draw upon. If I constantly go back to the basics, I can better maintain control and still enjoy life.

"We demolish arguments and every pretension that sets itself up against the knowledge of God, and we take captive every thought to make it obedient to Christ."
II Corinthians 10:5

Functional Atheists

On a cold winter day, an owner came to my kennel to drop off his dog. He didn't have the dog on a leash, believing his dog would listen to him. He was wrong. The dog took off. It was blowing snow and the wind chill was fierce. This dog had his own ideas on how to behave, which included ignoring his master and heading toward the road and traffic. Fortunately, the owner managed to chase the dog down and get the dog on leash.

Once I heard that when people run about on their own, denying God's part in our lives, we are functional atheists. This made me think. I have been so like this dog – wandering around, doing my own thing, ignoring my Master. I've come so close to being hit on the road it isn't funny. I've been thankful when God reeled me in and I was safely attached to his side again.

Maya the Cage Protective Mutt

Sometimes, a dog in the kennel is cage protective. Such was the case with Maya, a shepherd mix. When I walked by her kennel run, she barked aggressively, lunged at me, or jumped wildly against the door. It was a frightening sight. I'm glad I was familiar with this behavior. It would have scared me to death if I didn't know that the behavior stops as soon as the door opens.

It's true. As soon as I flip the latch and open the door, Maya usually walks out, tail wagging. That need to protect "her space" is gone.

I keep people at a distance until I know them well. Once I trust them, they're in. I don't worry about keeping up my guard. Some people are excessively protective. They bark louder. They lunge more aggressively. Trusting another person is very hard.

How can we open the doors of our heart to God? If people, who are visible and tangible, have hurt us, what will God do? Besides, some of God's people are the worst representatives of what God is really like.

Jesus stands at the door and knocks. He has good gifts for us. It's safe to open that door to God. If we open that door, we'll find peace. There's no reason to protect what God already understands and cares for better than we can - our hearts.

"Ask and it will be given to you; seek and you will find; knock and the door will be opened to you. For everyone who asks receives,; he who seeks finds; and to him who knocks, the door will be opened."
Matthew 7: 7-8

Unconcerned

There once was a dog in my kennel whose owner was extremely ill. It was an emergency call, and a friend dropped off the dog. I didn't hear anything from the owners or the friends for two weeks. Fortunately, in a small town, I managed to keep updated on how the owner was.

The dog, a happy Labrador, seemed unconcerned. He was happy to see me when I let him out, eagerly ran back to his cage for his meal, and chased a ball with gusto. He even took a dip in the pond.

He seemed to know that someone would be back for him.

I wish I had that kind of trust in God. I can't see Him. I have no idea where He is or what He's doing. I get a little concerned when I look at my odd surroundings. Yet, He is always with me and He knows where I am. Despite chaos all around, He does know what he's doing – in my life, in yours, in the world.

GOLDEN OLDIE

I have a soft spot for old dogs. Everyone coos over puppies but give me the old grey face of a seasoned dog any day over those little poop machines.

When I see an old dog, walking slowly, I think of all that it has been through with its owner. Did the dog grow up with the kids? Did the dog comfort its owner through divorce or death? Perhaps the dog was the confidante, the loyal friend that served a very specific function for their owner's stage of life. When these aged dogs pass on, we grieve not only the loss of our friend but also every thing that happened in our lives with that dog. Our secrets and our laughter die with our furred friend.

As I move through the phases of my life, I have seen friends come and go. It has given me great comfort to know that the Lord is always with me. He knows all of my pain, secrets, joys, dreams, and aspirations. His loyalty is unfailing. He is a true confidante. He delights in my laughter and accomplishments. He loves and forgives me through every shortcoming. He picks me up and moves me along after I fall.

Dogs, our temporary companions, point to a much bigger, more powerful force - our God. Dogs are just a shadow of what we can have with the Lord.

"The Lord is my shepherd, I shall not be in want.
He makes me lie down in green pastures, he leads me
beside quiet waters, he restores my soul. He guides
me in paths of righteousness for his name's sake. Even
though I walk through the valley of the shadow of
death, I will fear no evil, for you are with me."
Psalm 23:1-4

Rescued

There is a large network of dog lovers who rescue dogs from pounds across the country. They find them on the internet, complete adoption paperwork, and get them to the vet and on to a new home. Sometimes, they have to get the dog out of the pound quickly or the dog will be euthanized due to space limitations.

Occasionally, dogs are brought to my kennel until a volunteer can transport them to new homes. It's great to see such a network of people who care about the lives of these dogs. Some even make arrangements across the country, and into Canada. They sacrifice their time, their energy, travel expenses and wear and tear on their vehicles to save lives. When I see these dogs, I know they have truly had their life rescued. The dogs are unaware of these sacrifices or how close they came to death.

God has gone to extremes to save our lives too. It was a radical act to send His son to us. And he didn't get treated all that great either. But Jesus' act of obedience to his Father resulted in our lives being saved. His death was a sacrifice for each one of us. Many of us act unaware of this and live accordingly. If we stop to accept Jesus' life, death, and resurrection as truth, our lives can be transformed. Living out of gratitude for our saved lives will be a joy, not a burden.

> *"Jesus answered, 'I am the way the truth and the life. No one comes to the Father except through me. If you really knew me, you would know my Father as well. From now on, you do know him and have seen him."*
> John 14:6-7

The Dog Who Would be "King"

In the rural county in which I reside, the dog pound is almost always full. Thanks to a couple of dedicated employees and rescue groups, more dogs are getting adopted than ever before.

What's interesting to me is how far away these dogs may travel from their original rescue. For some reason, King was at the pound for a very long time. When the space was getting tight, King was in danger of being sent off to be euthanized. A rescue worker arranged for a rescue group, hundreds of miles away, to accept King. A series of volunteers got King to his new foster home.

When King became available for adoption in this new location, a family fell in love with him. He was just what they were looking for. King now lives in a multi-million dollar estate.

The coolest thing about God is He finds us in the most unlikely of places. He desires to take our tired, beat up, stinky selves and give us a mansion to live in with him. It doesn't matter if we come from a poor or rich family or what kind of a life we've led. God wants to adopt us all.

His love is open to everyone. All we need to do is choose to follow Him.

"Fear not for I have redeemed you; I have summoned you by name; you are mine. When you pass through the waters, I will be with you; when you pass through the rivers, they will not sweep over you. When you walk through the fire, you will not be burned; the flames will not set you ablaze. For I am the Lord your God, the Holy One of Israel, your Savior."

"Forget the former things; do not dwell on the past. See, I am doing a new thing! Now it springs up; do you not perceive it? I am making a way in the desert and streams in the wasteland."

Isaiah 43:1-3; 18-19

AND ONE FOR THE KITTEN

Living out in the country and being an animal lover means having lots of cats show up. A kitten not old enough to be away from its mother was once dropped off. I heard its mewing, and I used the universal kitty language of "here kitty kitty." Immediately, a tiny grey fluff ball bounded across the yard to me.

The orphan was covered in fleas, maggots and ring worm. Obviously, she had been terribly neglected. She was a mess. And she was chilled to the bone. I took her into my home and ran her tiny body under warm water. As the filth ran off her, she didn't fight the bath, she began to purr. She fit in the palm of my hand.

I thought of how God holds us in the palm of His hand, dealing with our filth, and loving us the whole time. It blew me away. Certainly, there is no safer place to be.

That kitten, Carbon, lives a great life here. She saunters around like a princess. She acts completely secure - like she knows she is loved.

"See, I have engraved you
on the palms of my hands."
Isaiah 49:16

ACKNOWLEDGEMENTS

This book was inspired by dogs and strife. It's hard to be thankful for all of it. I'm grateful Darren and I learned through the parallels of dog training and following God. These stories would not have made it to paper without many, many wonderful friends.

Two dear friends, Carole Siekerman and Chris Lyle, didn't live to see the final product but they read early drafts in spite of their own obstacles and learning curves.

Thanks to Karen Ward, who helped with photography before she even unpacked from her vacation.

I especially wish to thank Marilyn Nelson and Sue Fitzgerald who offered accurate editing and fantastic sarcasm.

And a special thanks to Ellie Miller, mother and artist extraordinaire.

Comments and questions are welcome at
dingodevotionals@yahoo.com

WRESTLE UP

by Lynne Scott

In college, my husband, Darren, was known as a powerful varsity wrestler. But wrestling became a distant memory just a few short years after he hung up his singlet. "It was a lifetime ago," he'd say. A year after we married, a menacing challenger entered our lives. This opponent would prove to be his toughest.

As a young wrestler, Darren lost nearly every match. He became familiar with the ceiling lights of gyms around the area, pinned under his opponent. This vantage point motivated him to fight back. With each, he improved. He lifted weights and attended summer camps. He wrestled his older brother. He wrestled his older sister (his most worthy opponent). He got better. By his senior year of high school, he set records and qualified twice for the state tournament.

The stratified weight classes used in wrestling insure safety and fairness, at least on paper. However, a lighter wrestler can opt to "wrestle up" to a heavier weight class. In a practice setting, nothing is at stake. In a meet, a loss lessens both the individual's record and the team's overall point score.

In college, Darren became the man to beat. During practices, he out wrestled everyone in and around his weight class - 134 pounds. So, he began to wrestle up, further testing his skills and challenging his muscles. If a teammate actually beat him in practice, Darren demanded the guy stay and wrestle him again, just to prove the win was a fluke. He even wrestled the heavy weights, who were over 190 pounds.

If a wrestling meet was coming up and Darren had previously beaten the opponent in his weight class, he'd wrestle up to a heavier weight class, jeopardizing his sparkling record and making his coaches tense. Darren knew the only way to beat the best was to risk a loss. He wasn't satisfied playing it safe. He believed that if you're going to lose, lose trying to win.

Each meet brought Darren closer to his goal of competing at the national tournament. He went all out for the full seven minutes of each match. He didn't dance around his opponent or hang on just to stall. By the third period, when most wrestlers tired, Darren hit his stride.

He believed in wrestling strong and healthy. In his book, starving to cut weight ultimately made the wrestler weaker. With naturally good metabolism, his body fat ratio was less than five percent.

Darren cross trained, punching a boxing heavy bag at his parents' home. Since he couldn't fit a bag of that size in his dorm room, he turned his mattress on its side and punched it. He pushed himself with extra workouts, running wind sprints up and down bleachers while carrying a weighted backpack over his shoulders. When bleachers weren't available, he adapted. Darren, wearing a weight-stuffed backpack, was running the stairs in the athletic building when the football coach first met him. The coach thought Darren was crazy until he learned Darren was training for the national championship.

Darren went to the Division III National Championships as a college junior in 1986. As he moved up the brackets in competition, he met a popular contender. When Darren's opponent took off his warm up sweats, even Darren's team coach was impressed by his imposing physique, commenting, "Wow, he's big. What are you going to do?" Despite the close match, Darren placed fifth. His opponent went on to win the national championship.

The next year, Darren was back. Darren met the same foe who had gone on to win the title the previous year.

But this time they met in the finals. Darren's opponent represented a prestigious university while no college in Darren's athletic conference had ever won a national championship.

As returning champion, the crowd cheered against Darren. But charismatic Darren had a significant following as well. The first two periods were scored a dead heat. Then, Darren got a bad call, putting him behind by one point.

Uncharacteristically, the fans booed loudly and even threw cups and other debris onto the mat. Several minutes passed as the litter was cleared. Despite the unfair call, Darren buckled down to return to the fight. But something had changed. The underdog, Darren, became the crowd favorite. His energy surged and soon he resumed attack mode.

When the third period buzzer sounded, the referee raised Darren's hand. The cheers of the crowd filled the air.

Darren stood on the top of the platform, the 1987 Division III National Champion for the 134 pound weight class. What foe couldn't be vanquished with such a victory?

After graduation, Darren worked at our alma mater's Admissions office. I joined the staff a year later. Even though our college school years overlapped, I didn't know Darren. And I certainly didn't know anything about wrestling. "Weren't you, like, the county champion or something?" I asked when we first met. This playful insult was nothing to him. He had a healthy ego and could take it. Two years later, we married.

Darren continued to work out like he was in training. He loved it. I realized that if I wanted to spend time with him, I better work out too. I even tried wind sprints, once. I also learned (the hard way) not to try to keep up with his eating as my metabolism wasn't as quick as his.

He soon noticed that one of his legs felt sluggish when he ran. By summer 1992, Darren's left thigh had shrunk an inch and a half. He visited a variety of doctors and underwent test after test. The diagnosis took two years and by Christmas of 1994, Darren's ailment had a very long name – Amyotrophic Lateral Sclerosis (ALS), more commonly known as Lou Gehrig's disease.

Most people with ALS die in 2-3 years. Darren had already survived beyond that. Our hopes of a long life together evaporated. When we learned his illness was genetic, our prospects of having children were gone as well.

In just five years, we went from being newlyweds to acting as if we were a retired couple. Not knowing how much time we'd have, we decided to reduce stress and increase fun. We quit our jobs and bought an RV, seeking refuge in a warm Florida winter. But ALS had followed us. Things most people take for granted, like unscrewing the top of a toothpaste tube, became difficult for Darren. After much soul searching, we returned to Ohio and sold the RV. We put down roots and started a home business.

Darren was selected to carry the Olympic torch as part of its national relay in 2002. When interviewed about this honor, he said, "I've got that mentality where I've got to bust my tail for however long I have, and do the best I can. I can't sit and whine about a bad call. I've got to keep pushing forward, and that is what I've chosen to do. I've been fully blessed that I've been given not just seven minutes, but a little overtime, too."

Wrestling wasn't the only area where he practiced his philosophy of "wrestling up." It influenced his whole life. Before ALS, Darren was content with a nominal faith. His diagnosis challenged every notion he'd ever had of God. There were very dark times, but he survived the fires. His faith became more refined. Like a champion, Darren kept attacking when doubt surfaced time and time again. He demanded answers. Sometimes he received understanding. Other times questions went unanswered. Even with doubts, he grew in faith.

Gradually, work around our country home became my responsibility. If I couldn't do it, Darren lined up someone who could. Within five years, Darren was so weak that he relied on me to help him stand and to get in and out of our vehicles. The time came when I gave him a piggy back ride to get upstairs at night.

Darren died July 26, 2003. Nearly eight hundred people attended his memorial service. In his 39 years, Darren touched countless lives. Because of his positive attitude, he received invitations to address civic, church and school groups. While he didn't consider himself a motivational speaker, his message and spirit resonated with the audience.

By his example, Darren taught that dancing around life's challenges wasn't an option. Winning by stalling and merely holding on is an empty victory. Darren's life showed the importance of improving one's strength in order to take on new ventures, no matter how risky.

Now I want to gain strength and take on new ventures even though it can be risky. Like Darren, I want to meet people who will challenge my faith, intellect, and wit. I want to do things in my life that aren't considered safe and reasonable on paper. At times, I may lose. But I will lose trying to win. I want to wrestle up.

Lynne and Foster at home

About the Author

LYNNE SCOTT has operated Good Shepherd Boarding Kennel on the Gold Coast of Hardin County, Ohio since 1998. She has served as a Children's Leader and Secretary for Bible Study Fellowship, taught Sunday school, and leads a local multi-denominational Bible study. Lynne also is a founding member of ReStore Community Center in Ada, Ohio. In addition to *Dingo Devotionals*, she has written two screenplays.

About the Illustrator

ELLIE MILLER has been Lynne's mother since 1966. She lives in Toledo, Ohio where she is a member of Toledo Women's Art League, Northwest Ohio Watercolor Society, and an Associate member of the Ohio Watercolor Society. She also has a son, Todd.

CPSIA information can be obtained
at www.ICGtesting.com
Printed in the USA
FFOW03n2227180917
40103FF

9 781434 331533